MW01701923

UpwardAction LLC

Name: ____

Business Name: ________________________________

Date: ____

FaithFocusFlow.com

My Daily Walk with Christ: A Journal for Christian Business Owners and Leaders

Published by UpwardAction® Media, a division of Upward Action LLC
www.UpwardActionMedia.com | www.FaithFocusFlow.com

FaithFocusFlow.com is the Christian education and training division of Upward Action LLC.

This book is available at quantity discounts for bulk purchases. For information email WeCare@UpwardAction.com or call (800) 753-6576.

ISBN: 978-0-9912536-9-2

FAITHFOCUSFLOW.COM

You will call to me and come and pray to me,
and I will listen to you.

You will seek me and find me when you search for me with all your heart.

Jeremiah 29:12-13

FaithFocusFlow.com

A letter from TC Cooper - founder of Faith Focus Flow™ - about how to use your "My Daily Walk with Christ" business journal.

* * * * *

Dear Christianpreneur or Business Leader ~

This "My Daily Walk with Christ" business journal is designed to help busy people who love the Lord, like you, do business with and for God.

I created the first version of this journal in a 3-ring binder to help me do three things: (i) focus on the important parts of building, maintaining and growing my business, (ii) submit every business idea to God in prayer and, most importantly, (iii) wait for God's divine direction before taking action.

Prior to "My Daily Walk with Christ," here's what commonly happened in my business ... I'd get a great idea and write it down on whatever notepad I had handy. Soon after, I'd go into planning mode, writing out SMART goals to make things happen. Once my goals were established, I'd pray about my plans, asking God to bless my actions and align my will with His purpose.

Here's the problem with this approach ... by the time I incorporated God into my plans, I was already in action and as my grandparents would say ... the horse was out of the gate. This inefficient approach to business planning resulted in lost time, money and opportunities to serve.

About a year ago, I changed my approach, and this shift has transformed my business from the inside out. Instead of praying to God when implementing my plans, I began aligning my thoughts with God's Word and purpose for my life at the start of every idea. This change resulted in a 5-Step process I've used to design the "My Daily Walk with Christ" business journal.

Step One: Study, and have FAITH in God's Holy Word.

All Scripture is breathed out by God and profitable for teaching, for reproof, for correction, and for training in righteousness, that the man of God may be competent, equipped for every good work.

2 Timothy 3:16-17

During my shift, I developed the discipline of dedicating a portion of my morning bible study to asking God to give me wisdom in building, managing and growing particular aspects of my business. God responded by giving me topics to integrate into my study, which led to specific passages of scripture. I call this process of applying biblical principles to business planning "walking with Christ."

Thanks to Holy Spirit's guidance, every entry in this journal has a section for writing down bible verses to support your "walk with Christ" in thinking through and developing your business ideas. If you need help identifying scripture, use our "My Daily Walk Through Scripture" reading plans to get started! There's one at the start of every one of our journals.

Step Two: FOCUS, then write.

Let your eyes look directly forward, and your gaze be straight before you.
Proverbs 4:25

During the journey of being intentional about writing down ideas in order to prayerfully bring them to life, I've found it helpful to connect every idea to a specific business solution and focus. Being intentional about doing this helps make ideas captive to God and in service to our Christ-centered business. Use this journal to (i) write down your ideas as they come to you and (ii) connect them to a specific solution and focal point in your business.

Step Three: Pray, then let your ideas FLOW.

But seek first the kingdom of God and his righteousness
and all these things will be added to you.
Matthew 6:33

Once you have some clarity about your ideas as shaped by scripture, and you've connected your ideas to a particular business solution and focal point, it's a great time to submit what you've written to the Lord for divine wisdom and instruction. Ask God to order your steps. Write down whatever God reveals to you. Let scripture guide your interpretation of what you're hearing from God.

If any of you lacks wisdom, you should ask God, who gives generously to all without finding fault, and it will be given to you.
James 1:5

Be intentional and specific in your prayers, so you can be most aware of when and how God responds to you. Take nothing for granted; pay attention to every single thing in your environment. Know there are no consequences, only divine directions, instructions and whispers from God. All things are working for you. Write down whatever you sense.

FAITHFOCUSFLOW.COM

Step Four: Get clear about your next steps.

Your word is a lamp for my feet, a light on my path.
Psalm 119:105

Think about what God revealed during your prayer time and write down what He says is next. Perhaps you need to do more research to fully develop an idea. If so, start a new journal entry with your refined ideas. Or, perhaps God has given you clearance to put your ideas into action. Write out your next steps, which should include grabbing your "My SMART Action Plan" planner to align your ideas with your vision and monthly objectives, and then create SMART Goals. Get your planner at www.smartgoalsplanner.com.

Step Five: Praise, then pray.

Before ending your business planning time with the Lord, it's important to exercise your faith through praise and prayer.

Is anyone among you suffering? Let him pray.
Is anyone cheerful? Let him sing praise.
James 5:13

Develop a practice of writing down at least three things for which you are grateful (it's okay to repeat) and at least a few words or sentences of prayer at the end of every journal entry. Start-with praise and gratitude, end with prayer.

* * * * * *

Here's what I know: God's plans for you and what your business can accomplish for His kingdom are beyond anything you could ever imagine, plan or create by yourself.

For I know the plans I have for you," declares the Lord,
"plans to prosper you and not to harm you, plans to give you hope and a future."
Jeremiah 29:11

Tap into God's wisdom at the start of every idea and be ready to quantum leap into building, maintaining and growing a business that honors God, supports people and builds wealth. Let us know if Team Faith Focus Flow™ can help. We love you.

Your Sister in Christ ~

Tasha "TC" Cooper
Founder of Faith Focus Flow™

FAITHFOCUSFLOW.COM

My Daily Walk through Scripture - Morning Glory Edition

80 Bible Passages to Help You:
* Strengthen Your Prayer Life * Increase Your Obedience *
* Ignite Your Worship * Empower Your Walk *

Every version of the "**My Daily Walk with Christ**" business journal has a different theme and contains a unique collection of suggested bibles passages that we call "**My Daily Walk through Scripture**."

The theme for this version of the journal is "**Morning Glory**." It's my prayer that you'll find several passages in this collection of scripture that speak to your heart, enhance your use of this journal and, most especially, strengthen your personal walk with Christ.

~ TC Cooper, Founder of Faith Focus Flow ™

Scripture to Strengthen Your Prayer Life	Scripture to Increase Your Obedience
☐ Psalm 34:15	☐ Exodus 19:5
☐ 1 Chronicles 16:11	☐ John 14:23-24
☐ Daniel 10:12	☐ Deuteronomy 11:13-14
☐ Mark 9:23-24	☐ James 1:22-25
☐ Psalm 4:3	☐ 2 Corinthians 10:4-5
☐ Romans 8:26	☐ Proverbs 10:7
☐ James 5:13	☐ Romans 2:6-8
☐ Job 22:17	☐ Luke 11:28
☐ Psalm 5:3	☐ Joshua 1:8
☐ Colossians 4:2	☐ 1 Kings 2:3
☐ 1 John 5:14-15	☐ Luke 10:27
☐ Luke 18:1	☐ Deuteronomy 28:14
☐ Daniel 9:18	☐ Acts 5:27-29
☐ Ephesians 6:18	☐ Zechariah 1:3,6
☐ Psalm 102:17	☐ Isaiah 1:19-20
☐ Romans 12:12	☐ Romans 12:2
☐ Jeremiah 29:12	☐ Luke 9:23
☐ James 4:3	☐ 1 Peter 4:12, 17, 18
☐ Matthew 26:41	☐ Deuteronomy 28:1-2
☐ Psalm 145:18-19	☐ Jeremiah 7:23

FAITHFOCUSFLOW.COM

Scripture to Ignite Your Worship	Scripture to Empower Your Walk
☐ Psalm 47:1-2	☐ Micah 6:8
☐ Daniel 4:37	☐ Leviticus 26:12
☐ John 4:23-24	☐ Deuteronomy 8:6-10
☐ Psalm 57-8	☐ Romans 1:16-17
☐ 2 Kings 17:35-36	☐ Zechariah 3:7
☐ Isaiah 25:1	☐ Psalm 119:3
☐ 2 Samuel 7:22	☐ Ephesians 2:10
☐ Daniel 2:20	☐ Deuteronomy 10:12-13
☐ Psalm 63:1	☐ 1 John 1:6-7
☐ Exodus 15:2	☐ Galatians 5:16
☐ Deuteronomy 10:21	☐ Psalm 128:1-2
☐ Romans 11:36	☐ John 8:12
☐ Psalm 75:1	☐ 2 Corinthians 6:16
☐ Isaiah 63:7	☐ Deuteronomy 26:16-19
☐ 1 Samuel 2:2	☐ 1 John 2:3-5
☐ 1 Chronicles 16:34	☐ Malachi 2:5-7
☐ Psalm 66:3-4	☐ 1 Samuel 2:30
☐ Psalm 66:5-6	☐ 1 Kings 3:9, 14
☐ Psalm 66:8-9	☐ Leviticus 26:3-7
☐ Matthew 4:8-11	☐ Deuteronomy 11:22-23

Join our #FaithFocusFlow community at www.FaithFocusFlow.com/eLetter for updates about new Bible Reading Plans for faith-based business owners and leaders.

You'll also receive our weekly eLetter filed with practical advise for businesses that honor God, serve people and build sustainable wealth.

FAITHFOCUSFLOW.COM

Connect with us on social media for social marketing and business development tips on our UpwardAction channels.

Facebook: www.Facebook.com/UpwardAction
Twitter: www.Twitter.com/UpwardAction
Instagram: www.Instagram.com/UpwardAction
Periscope: www.Periscope.TV/UpwardAction

Connect with us on social media for faith-based inspiration and bible-based devotionals.

Facebook: www.Facebook.com/FaithFocusFlow
Twitter: www.Twitter.com/FaithFocusFlow
Instagram: www.Instagram.com/FaithFocusFlow

FAITHFOCUSFLOW.COM

Jesus said to him, "If you can? Everything is possible for the one who believes."

Mark 9:23

FaithFocusFlow.com

Today is ______ , __________ , _________ , ______ **and it's** ________
(day) (month) (date) (year) (time)

Commit to the Lord whatever you do,
He will establish your plans.
Proverbs 16:3 (NIV)

Today, my walk with Christ is powered by _____________.
(scripture reference)

Business Focus:

My Thoughts: ____

____

____

____

____

____

____

____

____

____

____

____

____

____

FaithFocusFlow.com

Notes, Ideas & Plans:

FAITHFOCUSFLOW.COM

ASK & RECEIVE

I've prayed about my business focus and ...

FAITHFOCUSFLOW.COM

LISTEN & OBEY

Next Steps: ______________________________

Gratitude, Praise & Prayer

Write down 3 business-related things for which you are grateful and a business-focused request to the Lord for which you are prayerful.

FaithFocusFlow.com

Today is ______, ________, ________, ______ and it's _______

(day) (month) (date) (year) (time)

Rejoice always, pray continually, give thanks in all circumstances;
for this is God's will for you in Christ Jesus.
1 Thessalonians 5:16-18 (NIV)

Today, my walk with Christ is powered by ____________.

(scripture reference)

Business Focus:

My Thoughts: ______________________________

FAITHFOCUSFLOW.COM

Notes, Ideas & Plans:

FaithFocusFlow.com

ASK & RECEIVE

I've prayed about my business focus and ...

FAITHFOCUSFLOW.COM

LISTEN & OBEY

Next Steps: ___

Gratitude, Praise & Prayer

Write down 3 business-related things for which you are grateful and a business-focused request to the Lord for which you are prayerful.

FAITHFOCUSFLOW.COM

Today is ______ , ________ , ________ , ______ **and it's** ______
(day) (month) (date) (year) (time)

"For I know the plans I have for you," declares the LORD,
"plans to prosper you and not to harm you, plans to give you hope and a future."
Jeremiah 29:11 (NIV)

Today, my walk with Christ is powered by __________.
(scripture reference)

Business Focus:

My Thoughts: ____________________

FAITHFOCUSFLOW.COM

Notes, Ideas & Plans:

FaithFocusFlow.com

ASK & RECEIVE

I've prayed about my business focus and ...

FAITHFOCUSFLOW.COM

LISTEN & OBEY

Next Steps: ______________________________

Gratitude, Praise & Prayer

Write down 3 business-related things for which you are grateful and a business-focused request to the Lord for which you are prayerful.

FAITHFOCUSFLOW.COM

Today is ______ , __________ , _________ , ______ **and it's** ________

(day) (month) (date) (year) (time)

Great is the power of a good person's fervent prayer.
James 5:16 (OEB)

Today, my walk with Christ is powered by ______________.
(scripture reference)

Business Focus:

My Thoughts: ____

FAITHFOCUSFLOW.COM

Notes, Ideas & Plans:

FAITHFOCUSFLOW.COM

ASK & RECEIVE

I've prayed about my business focus and ...

FaithFocusFlow.com

LISTEN & OBEY

Next Steps:

Gratitude, Praise & Prayer

Write down 3 business-related things for which you are grateful and a business-focused request to the Lord for which you are prayerful.

Today is ______ , __________ , _________ , ______ **and it's** _______

(day) (month) (date) (year) (time)

May he grant you your heart's desire, and bring all your plans to pass.
Psalm 20:4 (OEB)

Today, my walk with Christ is powered by ____________.
(scripture reference)

Business Focus:

My Thoughts: ______________________________

Notes, Ideas & Plans:

FaithFocusFlow.com

ASK & RECEIVE

I've prayed about my business focus and ...

FAITHFOCUSFLOW.COM

LISTEN & OBEY

Next Steps:

Gratitude, Praise & Prayer

Write down 3 business-related things for which you are grateful and a business-focused request to the Lord for which you are prayerful.

FAITHFOCUSFLOW.COM

Today is ______ , _________ , ________ , ______ and it's ______

(day) (month) (date) (year) (time)

If you remain united to me, and my teaching remains in your hearts,
ask whatever you wish, and it will be yours.
It is by your bearing fruit plentifully, and so showing yourselves my disciples,
that my Father is honored.
John 15:7-9 (OEB)

Today, my walk with Christ is powered by ____________.

(scripture reference)

Business Focus:

My Thoughts: ____

FaithFocusFlow.com

Notes, Ideas & Plans:

FaithFocusFlow.com

ASK & RECEIVE

I've prayed about my business focus and ...

FAITHFOCUSFLOW.COM

LISTEN & OBEY

Next Steps:

Gratitude, Praise & Prayer

Write down 3 business-related things for which you are grateful and a business-focused request to the Lord for which you are prayerful.

FAITHFOCUSFLOW.COM

Today is ______, __________, _________, ______ **and it's** _______

(day) (month) (date) (year) (time)

In their hearts humans plan their course,
but the Lord establishes their steps.
Proverbs 16:9 (NIV)

Today, my walk with Christ is powered by ___________.
(scripture reference)

Business Focus:

My Thoughts: ____________________________________

FAITHFOCUSFLOW.COM

Notes, Ideas & Plans:

FAITHFOCUSFLOW.COM

ASK & RECEIVE

I've prayed about my business focus and ...

FaithFocusFlow.com

LISTEN & OBEY

Next Steps: ______________________________

Gratitude, Praise & Prayer

Write down 3 business-related things for which you are grateful and a business-focused request to the Lord for which you are prayerful.

FAITHFOCUSFLOW.COM

Today is ______ , __________ , ________ , ______ **and it's** _______

(day) (month) (date) (year) (time)

Suppose one of you wants to build a tower.
Won't you first sit down and estimate the cost
to see if you have enough money to complete it?
Luke 14:28 (NIV)

Today, my walk with Christ is powered by ____________.
(scripture reference)

Business Focus:

My Thoughts: ______________________________

FAITHFOCUSFLOW.COM

Notes, Ideas & Plans:

ASK & RECEIVE

I've prayed about my business focus and ...

FAITHFOCUSFLOW.COM

LISTEN & OBEY

Next Steps: ______________________________

Gratitude, Praise & Prayer

Write down 3 business-related things for which you are grateful and a business-focused request to the Lord for which you are prayerful.

FaithFocusFlow.com

Today is ______ , __________ , _________ , ______ and it's ________

(day) (month) (date) (year) (time)

And pray in the Spirit on all occasions with all kinds of prayers and requests.
Ephesians 6:18 (NIV)

Today, my walk with Christ is powered by ______________.

(scripture reference)

Business Focus:

My Thoughts: ____

Notes, Ideas & Plans:

FAITHFOCUSFLOW.COM

ASK & RECEIVE

I've prayed about my business focus and ...

FAITHFOCUSFLOW.COM

LISTEN & OBEY

Next Steps: ______________________________

Gratitude, Praise & Prayer

Write down 3 business-related things for which you are grateful and a business-focused request to the Lord for which you are prayerful.

FaithFocusFlow.com

Today is ______ , __________ , _________ , ______ **and it's** ________
(day) (month) (date) (year) (time)

Let me learn of your love in the morning, for my trust is in you.
Teach me the way I should go: for my heart longs for you.
Psalm 143:8 (OEB)

Today, my walk with Christ is powered by ______________.
(scripture reference)

Business Focus:

My Thoughts: ____

FAITHFOCUSFLOW.COM

Notes, Ideas & Plans:

FAITHFOCUSFLOW.COM

ASK & RECEIVE

I've prayed about my business focus and ...

FAITHFOCUSFLOW.COM

LISTEN & OBEY

Next Steps: ______________________________

Gratitude, Praise & Prayer

Write down 3 business-related things for which you are grateful and a business-focused request to the Lord for which you are prayerful.

Today is ______ , __________ , __________ , _______ and it's ________

(day) (month) (date) (year) (time)

Plans fail for lack of counsel, but with many advisers they succeed.
Proverbs 15:22 (NIV)

Today, my walk with Christ is powered by _______________.
(scripture reference)

Business Focus:

My Thoughts: ____

FAITHFOCUSFLOW.COM

Notes, Ideas & Plans:

ASK & RECEIVE

I've prayed about my business focus and ...

LISTEN & OBEY

Next Steps: ______________________

Gratitude, Praise & Prayer

Write down 3 business-related things for which you are grateful and a business-focused request to the Lord for which you are prayerful.

FAITHFOCUSFLOW.COM

Today is ______ , __________ , _________ , ______ and it's _______

(day) (month) (date) (year) (time)

When praying, do not repeat the same words over and over again, as is done by the Gentiles, who think that by using many words they will obtain a hearing. Do not imitate them; for God, your Father, knows what you need before you ask him.
Matthew 6:7-9 (OEB)

Today, my walk with Christ is powered by ____________.
(scripture reference)

Business Focus:

My Thoughts: ____________________________________

FaithFocusFlow.com

Notes, Ideas & Plans:

FAITHFOCUSFLOW.COM

ASK & RECEIVE

I've prayed about my business focus and ...

FaithFocusFlow.com

LISTEN & OBEY

Next Steps: ______________________________

Gratitude, Praise & Prayer

Write down 3 business-related things for which you are grateful and a business-focused request to the Lord for which you are prayerful.

FaithFocusFlow.com

Today is ______ , __________ , _________ , ______ **and it's** _______
(day) (month) (date) (year) (time)

Do not wear yourself out to get rich; do not trust your own cleverness.
Proverbs 23:4 (NIV)

Today, my walk with Christ is powered by ____________.
(scripture reference)

Business Focus:

My Thoughts: ____

FaithFocusFlow.com

Notes, Ideas & Plans:

FaithFocusFlow.com

ASK & RECEIVE

I've prayed about my business focus and ...

FAITHFOCUSFLOW.COM

LISTEN & OBEY

Next Steps: ______________________________

Gratitude, Praise & Prayer

Write down 3 business-related things for which you are grateful and a business-focused request to the Lord for which you are prayerful.

FaithFocusFlow.com

Today is ______ , __________ , _________ , ______ **and it's** _______
(day) (month) (date) (year) (time)

Do not be anxious about anything,
but in every situation, by prayer and petition, with thanksgiving,
present your requests to God.
Philippians 4:6 (NIV)

Today, my walk with Christ is powered by ____________.
(scripture reference)

Business Focus:

My Thoughts: ____

FaithFocusFlow.com

Notes, Ideas & Plans:

FaithFocusFlow.com

ASK & RECEIVE

I've prayed about my business focus and ...

LISTEN & OBEY

Next Steps: ______________________________

Gratitude, Praise & Prayer

Write down 3 business-related things for which you are grateful and a business-focused request to the Lord for which you are prayerful.

FAITHFOCUSFLOW.COM

Today is ______ , _________ , ________ , ______ and it's ______
(day) (month) (date) (year) (time)

Listen and hear my voice.
Pay attention and hear what I say.
Isaiah 28:23 (NIV)

Today, my walk with Christ is powered by ___________.
(scripture reference)

Business Focus:

My Thoughts: ____

FAITHFOCUSFLOW.COM

Notes, Ideas & Plans:

ASK & RECEIVE

I've prayed about my business focus and ...

LISTEN & OBEY

Next Steps: ______________________________

Gratitude, Praise & Prayer

Write down 3 business-related things for which you are grateful and a business-focused request to the Lord for which you are prayerful.

FaithFocusFlow.com

Today is ______ , __________ , _________ , ______ **and it's** _______
(day) (month) (date) (year) (time)

O teach us to count our days so our minds may learn wisdom. Psalm 90:12 (OEB)

Today, my walk with Christ is powered by ____________.
(scripture reference)

Business Focus:

My Thoughts: ____

FAITHFOCUSFLOW.COM

Notes, Ideas & Plans:

ASK & RECEIVE

I've prayed about my business focus and ...

LISTEN & OBEY

Next Steps: ______________________________

Gratitude, Praise & Prayer

Write down 3 business-related things for which you are grateful and a business-focused request to the Lord for which you are prayerful.

Today is _____ , _________ , ________ , ______ **and it's** _______

(day) (month) (date) (year) (time)

I sought the LORD, and he answered me;
he delivered me from all my fears.
Psalm 34:4 (NIV)

Today, my walk with Christ is powered by ___________.
(scripture reference)

Business Focus:

My Thoughts: ______________________________

FaithFocusFlow.com

Notes, Ideas & Plans:

ASK & RECEIVE

I've prayed about my business focus and ...

FAITHFOCUSFLOW.COM

LISTEN & OBEY

Next Steps: ______________________________

Gratitude, Praise & Prayer

Write down 3 business-related things for which you are grateful and a business-focused request to the Lord for which you are prayerful.

FAITHFOCUSFLOW.COM

Today is ______ , __________ , _________ , ______ **and it's** _______

(day) (month) (date) (year) (time)

Draw near to God and He will draw near to you.
James 4:8 (OEB)

Today, my walk with Christ is powered by ___________.

(scripture reference)

Business Focus:

My Thoughts: ______________________________

FAITHFOCUSFLOW.COM

Notes, Ideas & Plans:

FaithFocusFlow.com

ASK & RECEIVE

I've prayed about my business focus and ...

LISTEN & OBEY

Next Steps: ______________________________

Gratitude, Praise & Prayer

Write down 3 business-related things for which you are grateful and a business-focused request to the Lord for which you are prayerful.

FAITHFOCUSFLOW.COM

Today is ______ , __________ , _________ , ______ **and it's** _______

(day) (month) (date) (year) (time)

May God make you perfect in everything that is good, so that you may be able to do his will.
May he bring out in us all that is pleasing in his sight, through Jesus Christ,
to whom be all glory for ever and ever. Amen.
Hebrews 13:21 (OEB)

Today, my walk with Christ is powered by ____________.
(scripture reference)

Business Focus:

My Thoughts: ____

____

____

____

____

____

____

____

____

____

____

____

____

____

FAITHFOCUSFLOW.COM

Notes, Ideas & Plans:

ASK & RECEIVE

I've prayed about my business focus and ...

FAITHFOCUSFLOW.COM

LISTEN & OBEY

Next Steps: ____________________________

Gratitude, Praise & Prayer

Write down 3 business-related things for which you are grateful and a business-focused request to the Lord for which you are prayerful.

FAITHFOCUSFLOW.COM

Today is ______ , __________ , _________ , ______ **and it's** ________
(day) (month) (date) (year) (time)

Your kingdom come, your will be done, on earth as it is in heaven.
Matthew 6:10 (OEB)

Today, my walk with Christ is powered by ____________.
(scripture reference)

Business Focus:

My Thoughts: ____

FaithFocusFlow.com

Notes, Ideas & Plans:

FaithFocusFlow.com

ASK & RECEIVE

I've prayed about my business focus and ...

LISTEN & OBEY

Next Steps: ______________________________

Gratitude, Praise & Prayer

Write down 3 business-related things for which you are grateful and a business-focused request to the Lord for which you are prayerful.

Today is ______ , ________ , ________ , ______ **and it's** ______

(day) (month) (date) (year) (time)

And in union with him, and through our trust in him,
we find courage to approach God with confidence.
Ephesians 3:12-13 (OEB)

Today, my walk with Christ is powered by __________.

(scripture reference)

Business Focus:

My Thoughts: ______________________________

FaithFocusFlow.com

Notes, Ideas & Plans:

ASK & RECEIVE

I've prayed about my business focus and ...

LISTEN & OBEY

Next Steps: ______________________________

Gratitude, Praise & Prayer

Write down 3 business-related things for which you are grateful and a business-focused request to the Lord for which you are prayerful.

FAITHFOCUSFLOW.COM

Today is ______ , __________ , _________ , ______ **and it's** _______

(day) (month) (date) (year) (time)

But, when one of you prays, they should go into their own room,
shut the door, and pray to their Father who dwells in secret;
and their Father, who sees what is secret, will reward them.
Matthew 6:6-7 (OEB)

Today, my walk with Christ is powered by ____________.
(scripture reference)

Business Focus:

My Thoughts: ______________________________

FaithFocusFlow.com

Notes, Ideas & Plans:

ASK & RECEIVE

I've prayed about my business focus and ...

LISTEN & OBEY

Next Steps: ___

Gratitude, Praise & Prayer

Write down 3 business-related things for which you are grateful and a business-focused request to the Lord for which you are prayerful.

FAITHFOCUSFLOW.COM

Today is ______ , __________ , _________ , ______ and it's ________
(day) (month) (date) (year) (time)

If God is on our side, who can there be against us?
God did not withhold his own Son, but gave him up on behalf of us all;
will he not, then, with him, freely give us all things?
Romans 8:31-32 (OEB)

Today, my walk with Christ is powered by ____________.
(scripture reference)

Business Focus:

My Thoughts: ____

____

____

____

____

____

____

____

____

____

____

____

____

____

FAITHFOCUSFLOW.COM

Notes, Ideas & Plans:

ASK & RECEIVE

I've prayed about my business focus and ...

FAITHFOCUSFLOW.COM

LISTEN & OBEY

Next Steps: ______________________________

Gratitude, Praise & Prayer

Write down 3 business-related things for which you are grateful and a business-focused request to the Lord for which you are prayerful.

FAITHFOCUSFLOW.COM

Today is ______ , __________ , __________ , _______ **and it's** ________
(day) (month) (date) (year) (time)

As the heavens are higher than the earth, so are my ways higher than your ways and my thoughts than your thoughts.
Isaiah 55:9 (NIV)

Today, my walk with Christ is powered by ____________.
(scripture reference)

Business Focus:

My Thoughts: ____

FAITHFOCUSFLOW.COM

Notes, Ideas & Plans:

ASK & RECEIVE

I've prayed about my business focus and ...

FAITHFOCUSFLOW.COM

LISTEN & OBEY

Next Steps: ______________________________

Gratitude, Praise & Prayer

Write down 3 business-related things for which you are grateful and a business-focused request to the Lord for which you are prayerful.

FaithFocusFlow.com

Today is _____ , _________ , ________ , ______ and it's _______

(day) (month) (date) (year) (time)

Jesus looked hard at them and said,
"No chance at all if you think you can pull it off yourself.
Every chance in the world if you trust God to do it."
Matthew 19:26 (MSG)

Today, my walk with Christ is powered by ____________.

(scripture reference)

Business Focus:

My Thoughts: ____

____

____

____

____

____

____

____

____

____

____

____

____

____

FAITHFOCUSFLOW.COM

Notes, Ideas & Plans:

ASK & RECEIVE

I've prayed about my business focus and ...

FaithFocusFlow.com

LISTEN & OBEY

Next Steps: ______________________________

Gratitude, Praise & Prayer

Write down 3 business-related things for which you are grateful and a business-focused request to the Lord for which you are prayerful.

FAITHFOCUSFLOW.COM

Today is ______ , __________ , _________ , ______ **and it's** _______

(day) (month) (date) (year) (time)

But I pray to you, Lord, for a time of favor.
In your great love answer me; with your loyal help,
save me from sinking down in the mire.
Psalm 69:13-14 (OEB)

Today, my walk with Christ is powered by _____________.

(scripture reference)

Business Focus:

My Thoughts: ______________________________

Notes, Ideas & Plans:

FAITHFOCUSFLOW.COM

ASK & RECEIVE

I've prayed about my business focus and ...

FAITHFOCUSFLOW.COM

LISTEN & OBEY

Next Steps: ____________________

Gratitude, Praise & Prayer

Write down 3 business-related things for which you are grateful and a business-focused request to the Lord for which you are prayerful.

FAITHFOCUSFLOW.COM

Today is ______ , _________ , ________ , ______ and it's _______

(day) (month) (date) (year) (time)

Trust in the Lord with all your heart and lean not on your own understanding;
in all your ways submit to him, and he will make your paths straight.
Proverbs 3:5-6 (NIV)

Today, my walk with Christ is powered by ____________.
(scripture reference)

Business Focus:

My Thoughts: ____

Notes, Ideas & Plans:

ASK & RECEIVE

I've prayed about my business focus and ...

FaithFocusFlow.com

LISTEN & OBEY

Next Steps: ______________________________

Gratitude, Praise & Prayer

Write down 3 business-related things for which you are grateful and a business-focused request to the Lord for which you are prayerful.

Today is ______ , ________ , ________ , ______ and it's ______
(day) (month) (date) (year) (time)

In you, Lord my God, I put my trust. Psalm 25:1 (NIV)

Today, my walk with Christ is powered by ____________.
(scripture reference)

Business Focus:

My Thoughts: ____

FAITHFOCUSFLOW.COM

Notes, Ideas & Plans:

ASK & RECEIVE

I've prayed about my business focus and ...

LISTEN & OBEY

Next Steps: ______________________________

Gratitude, Praise & Prayer

Write down 3 business-related things for which you are grateful and a business-focused request to the Lord for which you are prayerful.

FaithFocusFlow.com

Today is ______ , __________ , _________ , ______ and it's _______
(day) (month) (date) (year) (time)

If any one of you lacks wisdom, they should ask wisdom from the God who gives freely to everyone without reproach, and it will be given to them. But they should ask with confidence, never doubting; for the person who doubts is like a wave of the sea driven here and there at the mercy of the wind. Such a person must not expect that they will receive anything from the Lord.
James 1:5-8 (OEB)

Today, my walk with Christ is powered by ____________.
(scripture reference)

Business Focus:

My Thoughts: ________________________________

FaithFocusFlow.com

Notes, Ideas & Plans:

FaithFocusFlow.com

ASK & RECEIVE

I've prayed about my business focus and ...

LISTEN & OBEY

Next Steps:

Gratitude, Praise & Prayer

Write down 3 business-related things for which you are grateful and a business-focused request to the Lord for which you are prayerful.

FaithFocusFlow.com

Today is ______ , __________ , _________ , ______ **and it's** _______

(day) (month) (date) (year) (time)

Here is a simple, rule of thumb guide for behavior:
Ask yourself what you want people to do for you,
then grab the initiative and do it for them.
Add up God's Law and Prophets and this is what you get.
Matthew 7:12 (MSG)

Today, my walk with Christ is powered by _____________.

(scripture reference)

Business Focus:

My Thoughts: ____

FAITHFOCUSFLOW.COM

Notes, Ideas & Plans:

ASK & RECEIVE

I've prayed about my business focus and ...

FaithFocusFlow.com

LISTEN & OBEY

Next Steps: ______________________________

Gratitude, Praise & Prayer

Write down 3 business-related things for which you are grateful and a business-focused request to the Lord for which you are prayerful.

FAITHFOCUSFLOW.COM

Today is ______ , __________ , _________ , ______ **and it's** ________

(day) (month) (date) (year) (time)

But you must, dear friends, build up your characters on the foundation of your most holy faith, pray under the guidance of the Holy Spirit, and keep within the love of God.
Jude 20-21 (OEB)

Today, my walk with Christ is powered by ____________.

(scripture reference)

Business Focus:

My Thoughts: ______________________________

FAITHFOCUSFLOW.COM

Notes, Ideas & Plans:

ASK & RECEIVE

I've prayed about my business focus and ...

FaithFocusFlow.com

LISTEN & OBEY

Next Steps:

Gratitude, Praise & Prayer

Write down 3 business-related things for which you are grateful and a business-focused request to the Lord for which you are prayerful.

Today is ______ , __________ , _________ , _______ and it's ________

(day) (month) (date) (year) (time)

My dear children, let's not just talk about love; let's practice real love.
This is the only way we'll know we're living truly, living in God's reality.
It's also the way to shut down debilitating self-criticism, even when there is something to it.
For God is greater than our worried hearts and knows more about us than we do ourselves.
1 John 3:18-20 (MSG)

Today, my walk with Christ is powered by _____________.

(scripture reference)

Business Focus:

My Thoughts: ____

FaithFocusFlow.com

Notes, Ideas & Plans:

FaithFocusFlow.com

ASK & RECEIVE

I've prayed about my business focus and …

FAITHFOCUSFLOW.COM

LISTEN & OBEY

Next Steps: ___

Gratitude, Praise & Prayer

Write down 3 business-related things for which you are grateful and a business-focused request to the Lord for which you are prayerful.

FAITHFOCUSFLOW.COM

Today is ______ , ________ , ________ , ______ **and it's** ______

(day) (month) (date) (year) (time)

Summing it all up, friends, I'd say you'll do best by filling your minds and meditating on things true, noble, reputable, authentic, compelling, gracious - the best, not the worst; the beautiful, not the ugly; things to praise, not things to curse.
Philippians 4:8-9 (MSG)

Today, my walk with Christ is powered by ____________.
(scripture reference)

Business Focus:

My Thoughts: ______________________________

____

____

____

____

____

____

____

____

____

____

____

____

____

FaithFocusFlow.com

Notes, Ideas & Plans:

FaithFocusFlow.com

ASK & RECEIVE

I've prayed about my business focus and ...

FAITHFOCUSFLOW.COM

LISTEN & OBEY

Next Steps: ______

Gratitude, Praise & Prayer

Write down 3 business-related things for which you are grateful and a business-focused request to the Lord for which you are prayerful.

FAITHFOCUSFLOW.COM

Today is ______ , __________ , _________ , ______ **and it's** ________

(day) (month) (date) (year) (time)

Not everyone who says to me 'Master! Master!' will enter the kingdom of heaven, but only he who does the will of my Father who is in heaven.
Matthew 7:21-22 (OEB)

Today, my walk with Christ is powered by ____________.
(scripture reference)

Business Focus:

My Thoughts: ____

____

____

____

____

____

____

____

____

____

____

____

____

____

FAITHFOCUSFLOW.COM

Notes, Ideas & Plans:

ASK & RECEIVE

I've prayed about my business focus and ...

LISTEN & OBEY

Next Steps: ______________________________

Gratitude, Praise & Prayer

Write down 3 business-related things for which you are grateful and a business-focused request to the Lord for which you are prayerful.

Today is ______ , __________ , _________ , ______ **and it's** _______

(day) (month) (date) (year) (time)

This is God's Message, the God who made earth, made it livable and lasting,
known everywhere as God: "Call to me and I will answer you,
I'll tell you marvelous and wondrous things that you could never figure out on your own.
Jeremiah 33:3 (MSG)

Today, my walk with Christ is powered by ____________.
(scripture reference)

Business Focus:

My Thoughts: ______________________________

FaithFocusFlow.com

Notes, Ideas & Plans: ______________________________

FaithFocusFlow.com

ASK & RECEIVE

I've prayed about my business focus and ...

FAITHFOCUSFLOW.COM

LISTEN & OBEY

Next Steps: ______________________

Gratitude, Praise & Prayer

Write down 3 business-related things for which you are grateful and a business-focused request to the Lord for which you are prayerful.

FaithFocusFlow.com

Today is ______, __________, _________, ______ **and it's** _______

(day) (month) (date) (year) (time)

Humble yourselves, therefore, under the mighty hand of God, so that he may exalt you in his good time, laying all your anxieties on him, for he makes you his care.
1 Peter 5:6-8 (MSG)

Today, my walk with Christ is powered by _____________.
(scripture reference)

Business Focus:

My Thoughts: ____

Notes, Ideas & Plans:

FaithFocusFlow.com

ASK & RECEIVE

I've prayed about my business focus and ...

FaithFocusFlow.com

LISTEN & OBEY

Next Steps: ______________________________

Gratitude, Praise & Prayer

Write down 3 business-related things for which you are grateful and a business-focused request to the Lord for which you are prayerful.

FaithFocusFlow.com

It's time to order re-order!

We pray that your "***My Daily Walk with Christ***"

business journal is a blessing to you!

Keep up the momentum of consulting God with your

every business decision in writing.

Head on over to **www.FaithFocusFlow.com**

to re-order your planner today!

FAITHFOCUSFLOW.COM

I believe Jesus knows the desires of my heart. I rejoice that Holy Spirit helps me petition God to align my ambition with His purpose for my business, so I am doing His will here on earth as it is in heaven.

~ Tasha "TC" Cooper

FAITHFOCUSFLOW.COM

Today is ______ , __________ , _________ , ______ **and it's** ________

(day) (month) (date) (year) (time)

He who is in you is greater than the one who is in the world.
1 John 4:4 (OEB)

Today, my walk with Christ is powered by ____________.
(scripture reference)

Business Focus:

My Thoughts: ______________________________

FAITHFOCUSFLOW.COM

Notes, Ideas & Plans:

FAITHFOCUSFLOW.COM

ASK & RECEIVE

I've prayed about my business focus and ...

FAITHFOCUSFLOW.COM

LISTEN & OBEY

Next Steps: ______________________________

Gratitude, Praise & Prayer

Write down 3 business-related things for which you are grateful and a business-focused request to the Lord for which you are prayerful.

FaithFocusFlow.com

Today is ______ , __________ , _________ , ______ **and it's** ________

(day) (month) (date) (year) (time)

Don't look for shortcuts to God. The market is flooded with surefire, easygoing formulas for a successful life that can be practiced in your spare time. Don't fall for that stuff, even though crowds of people do. The way to life - to God! - is vigorous and requires total attention.
Matthew 7:13-14 (MSG)

Today, my walk with Christ is powered by ______________.
(scripture reference)

Business Focus:

My Thoughts: ____

FAITHFOCUSFLOW.COM

Notes, Ideas & Plans:

FaithFocusFlow.com

ASK & RECEIVE

I've prayed about my business focus and ...

LISTEN & OBEY

Next Steps: ______________________________

Gratitude, Praise & Prayer

Write down 3 business-related things for which you are grateful and a business-focused request to the Lord for which you are prayerful.

FaithFocusFlow.com

Today is ______ , __________ , _________ , ______ **and it's** ________
(day) (month) (date) (year) (time)

Quiet down before God, be prayerful before him.
Don't bother with those who climb the ladder, who elbow their way to the top.
Psalm 37:7 (MSG)

Today, my walk with Christ is powered by _____________.
(scripture reference)

Business Focus:

My Thoughts: ____

FAITHFOCUSFLOW.COM

Notes, Ideas & Plans:

ASK & RECEIVE

I've prayed about my business focus and ...

FAITHFOCUSFLOW.COM

LISTEN & OBEY

Next Steps: ______________________________

Gratitude, Praise & Prayer

Write down 3 business-related things for which you are grateful and a business-focused request to the Lord for which you are prayerful.

FAITHFOCUSFLOW.COM

Today is ______ , __________ , _________ , ______ **and it's** ________
(day) (month) (date) (year) (time)

Whatever you have learned or received or heard from me, or seen in me -put it into practice. And the God of peace will be with you.
Philippians 4:9 (NIV)

Today, my walk with Christ is powered by _____________.
(scripture reference)

Business Focus:

My Thoughts: ______________________________

FaithFocusFlow.com

Notes, Ideas & Plans:

FaithFocusFlow.com

ASK & RECEIVE

I've prayed about my business focus and ...

LISTEN & OBEY

Next Steps: ____________________

Gratitude, Praise & Prayer

Write down 3 business-related things for which you are grateful and a business-focused request to the Lord for which you are prayerful.

FAITHFOCUSFLOW.COM

It's time to order your new journal!

Visit us online at
www.FaithFocusFlow.com
to order additional copies of this business journal and other bible-based business resources.

FaithFocusFlow.com

ABOUT THE AUTHOR

Tasha "TC" Cooper is an attorney, Amazon best-selling author and President of **UpwardAction®** – a digital publishing and online training company she launched to pursue her passion for social media advocacy as a business. She is also the founder of **Faith Focus Flow™** - an online movement that helps Christianpreneurs and business leaders integrate Jesus into every single aspect of their business.

TC has been recognized as a leader in social media marketing, self-publishing and building influential brands online. She developed for UpwardAction® Media clients the CooperZone™ Academies, which includes on-demand training for Twitter, LinkedIn, Live Streaming and Online Marketing. Her collective social media following exceeds 50,000 people who tune in for her expert, actionable advice.

TC's background reflects her deep respect for both formal and informal education. She graduated from Hampton University in 3 years (as a member of the *Honors College*) while doing things she loved - like hosting shows on her college radio station. She graduated from Columbia Law School (as a *Harlan Fiske Stone Scholar*), where she fell in-love with the people and energy of New York City, especially Harlem. TC is also a certified executive coach and has spent nearly two decades as a business attorney with experience in real-estate, intellectual property and social media. She became a self-taught social media marketing and digital branding consultant after spending too many hours and dollars to count on experiential learning, coaches, training programs and building her own Internet based businesses.

A teacher at heart, TC has used the blessings of her life experiences to teach thousands of lawyers, business owners and leaders how to use social media to increase impact, expand influence and diversify income. Through #FaithFocusFlow, her work has helped more than 10,000 people who follow the **Faith Focus Flow™** brand draw closer to Christ through books, electronic newsletters, business planners and social media.

Follow #FaithFocusFlow on Instagram at www.Instagram.com/FaithFocusFlow.

Visit www.TashaCooper.com to learn more about TC and her training schedule.

FAITHFOCUSFLOW.COM

ABOUT FAITH FOCUS FLOW ™

FaithFocusFlow™ bible-based business resources are designed to help busy leaders and business owners incorporate Jesus Christ into every aspect of their professional life by design, not happenstance. We are committed to helping you build, maintain and grow businesses that honor God, support people and build sustainable wealth.

Visit FaithFocusFlow.com/ReadingPlans for Christ-influenced business tip and tools, including new reading plans for business as they are developed. Follow us on Instagram at www.FaithFocusFlow.com/Instagram for daily inspiration through images and inspired text.

FAITHFOCUSFLOW.COM

SPECIAL THANKS!

A Daily Walk with Christ - A Journal for Christian Business Owners and Leaders is made possible through the guidance of Holy Spirit; support of my parents - Harmon and Jannie Cooper; wise counsel of our inner circle - Marenda, Willae, Sonya & DeLores; fellowship with my #WorshipAndWork family on Periscope - Inez, Casondra, E. Michelle, Kenneth, Brandon and Tora; and brilliance of Mario, who makes magic happen in our company everyday.

I appreciate each of you so very much for all you do to support the Faith Focus Flow™ mission of bringing business owners and leaders closer to Christ. ~ Love, TC

FAITHFOCUSFLOW.COM

Made in the USA
Monee, IL
17 March 2021

63107820R00104